Sincere thanks to Susanne Kennedy for her commitment to bringing the cookbook dream to life with exceptional wordsmith, planning and design skills.
Big thanks also to Juliana Hinton for her design work, and to Simone Riddle, from La Salsa Inglesa, for her ongoing recipe advice and troubleshooting. Similarly, this book would not have been realised without the wonderful recipes and stories of Doña Isabel Sanchez Perez and Doña Melida Ovalle de Ramirez and others in our community.

PLANTING A PATH FOR THE WATER & THE WIND. Copyright © 2017 by Highland Support Project. No part of this book may be used or reproduced in any manner whatsoever without the written permission. For information address Highland Support Project, P.O. Box 7185, Richmond, VA 23221

ISBN-13: 9780692952115
ISBN-10: 069295211X

Author
Guadalupe Ramirez

Writer/Editor
Susanne Kennedy

Design
Juliana Hinton

Editor
Ben Blevins

FIRST EDITION

PLANTING A PATH FOR THE WATER & THE WIND

A cookbook of traditional Maya and Guatemalan recipes and stories

Asociación de Mujeres del Altiplano
Guadalupe Ramirez

The material contained in this publication is copyrighted to Asociacion de Mujeres del Altiplano (AMA) and Highland Support Project. This book was first published in September, 2017.

TABLE OF CONTENTS

I. Introduction
Opening Words, Guadalupe Ramiréz — 5

II. Staples
- History
  - Maíz — 10
  - Beans — 11
  - Milpa and three sisters — 13
  - Nutrition and Amaranth — 14
- Recipes
  - Refried Beans — 15
  - Frijoles con Espinaca — 16
  - Atol de Elote — 19
- Stories
  - The Turkey and Pepian — 20
  - The Turkey and Quipil — 21
- Recipes
  - Pepian — 23
  - Chiles Rellenos — 24
- Stories
  - AMA's Sustainable Agriculture Project — 28

III. Planting
- History
  - Preparations and Rituals — 32
- Recipes
  - Wheat Tortillas — 34
  - Wheat and Exchanging bread — 37
  - Arroz Guatemalteco — 38
  - Mayra's Beef Broth — 41
- Stories
  - Agriculture, The Silk Belt — 42

IV. Mid Harvest
- History
  - Cutting the First Leaves — 46
- Recipes
  - Tamales — 48
  - Jocón — 51
  - Caldos and Soups — 54
  - Caldo de Platano — 57
  - Caldo de Res — 58
- Stories
  - Making Things Last — 60
- Recipes
  - Escabeche — 62
  - Curtidos Rapidos — 65
- Stories
  - Water — 66
  - How things fall apart — 67

TABLE OF CONTENTS

V Harvest

History	Tapizca	68
	Tortillas, A Celebration of Life	70
Recipes	Corn Tortillas	73
	Radish and Citrus salad	74
Stories	Estofado and Weddings	76
Recipes	Estofado	78
Stories	Cardinal Points, Hero Twins	81

VI Dulces

History	Cacao, Honey, Panela	84
Recipes	Mango Pudding	85
	Chocolate Banana Bread	86
Stories	Honey, The Royal Lady	89
Recipes	Chocobananas	90
	Canellitas de Leche	92
	Platanos en Gloria	93
	Easter Sweet Bread	95
	Miel del Garbanzo	96
Stories	Day of the Dead	98

VII Closing Words

Lunch and Connection	102
Recovering Food Security	105
AMA Sustainable Gardening	106
Partner with AMA	111

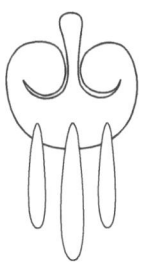

GUADALUPE RAMIRÉZ

[AMA FOUNDER]

I grew up in a rural Mam community in the western highlands of Guatemala. Today I live between the United States and my home country, directing the NGO, Asociacion de Mujeres del Altiplano (AMA), which I founded with my husband in the early 1990s. Since its inception, AMA has supported women and families in the hills surrounding San Marcos and Quetzaltenango through grassroots programming that builds resilience and independence. Our core programs teach women about behavioral health, preparing healthy, traditional meals, and support them to relearn sustainable agricultural practices, which were once habitual in their communities. This book was born from a number of impulses. Firstly, I wanted to share a beautiful vision of the world, an ancient template for leading an ethical and happy life, in part, because many aspects of this vision have an urgent relevance for the modern world. While most of the recipes contained in this book share stitches and threads with Spanish, Catholic and broader hybrid Guatemalan traditions, I am keen to convey the local Maya beliefs and rituals that are inseparable from these dishes in my community. Traditions that are intrinsically connected to the Maya cosmovision and are still strong in the Guatemalan fields and kitchens I wish to transport you to. It is indeed a miracle that many of these dishes and rituals are still prepared the same way they were centuries, or even millenniums, ago.

So, more than simply relaying cooking formulas or processes, it is my hope that this book will convey some of the attitudes and values I grew up with. Principles that the industrialized world can too easily fail to prioritize – namely, human connection, gratitude, or simply stopping to savor flavors, smells and company. The social fabric of my community continues to be woven and strengthened through unhurried lunches, and the words and wisdom that are shared between mouthfuls. This could once be said, I believe, about most social worlds. One constant, however, is that food habits always provide a window to the values, beliefs and priorities of a culture. I hope you enjoy this cookbook, and the picture it paints of a special world and it's relationship to food.

STAPLES

Beans, maíz, amaranth and squash - along with chili, cacao, avocados and platanos - have been key staple foods in the western highlands since these plants were domesticated by the Maya between 3,000 and 5,000 BC. The dog and turkey were also domesticated around this time, and the turkey continues to have strong culinary and cultural significance for many Indigenous people in Guatemala. These agricultural developments and domestications were also central to Mesoamericans' transition from a hunter-gatherer to a, more stationary, agriculturalist mode of existence.

MAÍZ
CORN

Maiz is not only a cornerstone of traditional and contemporary Mayan diets, it lies at the heart of many Indigenous rituals and beliefs. The Maya creation myth, as recounted in the Popul Vuh, tells how man was, ultimately, made from maíz after a number of unsuccessful attempts with clay, animals and wood. For this reason corn is sacred to the Maya, who believe it feeds both spirit and body and provides a connection to one's ancestors. Thus, deities were often depicted holding maíz or maíz leaves. And corn was frequently served at important festive and ceremonial events - some of which were simply about giving thanks, or asking, for a bountiful corn harvest. Corn became the principal staple in Mesoamerica, in part, because it was easy to dry, store and transport and, thus, use all year- round. Maíz was fundamental to Maya agricultural practices, particularly the Three Sisters and Milpa systems that have been practiced in Mesoamerica for thousands of years. The following two scholarly quotes, quickly lend perspective to how much Maya and Aztec cultures have influenced our modern dishes.

"Mesoamerica would deserve its place in the human pantheon if its inhabitants had only created maíz, in terms of harvest weight the world's most important crop. But the inhabitants of Mexico and northern Central America also developed tomatoes... all the world's squashes (except for a few domesticated in the United States); and many of the beans on dinner plates around the world. One writer estimates that Indians developed three-fifths of the crops now grown in cultivation, most of them in Mesoamerica. Having secured their food supply, the Mesoamerican societies turned to intellectual pursuits. In a millennium or less, a comparatively short time, they invented their own writing, astronomy and mathematics, including the zero." [1]

According to Jared Diamond, while "maíz is the most common domesticate, the common bean, tepary bean, scarlet runner bean, jicama, tomato all became common cultivates by 3500 BC." [2]

Maíz is still omnipresent in the Guatemalan diet, in the form of tortillas, tamales and atol, a hot beverage, which is offered as a comforting home remedy for most ailments.Recipes for these dishes can be found in this and later chapters which invite you to discover, or rediscover, the magic and versatility of maíz.

---

[1] (Mann, Charles C. 1491: Revelationsofthe Americas before Columbus. Vinton Press. 2005. Pages196–197)

[2] Diamond, Jared(1999). Guns, Germs and Steel: The Fates of Human Societies. New York: W W Norton & Co. ISBN0-393-31755-2

FRIJOLES
BEANS

The common bean most often found in Guatemala has the formal name of *Phaseolus vulgaris*. The bean provides a key source of vegetable protein in the contemporary Guatemalan diet and has performed this nutritional role in Maya civilizations since its domestication 5000 years ago. The much loved Guatemalan bean is also versatile. It can be found at all times of the day or night served refried, whole, or blended to a smooth paste, usually as a accompaniment to tortillas, bread, rice or eggs. Beans are a sturdy crop, which can be planted in the March-April or June-July windows. It takes between 100 to 140 days to grow depending on the variety.

ANCIENT PRACTICES
MILPA AND THE THREE SISTERS

The meaning of the term 'milpa' varies depending on the Maya cultural group or region. In parts of Mexico, such as the Yucatan, for instance, the term denotes a slash and burn, crop rotation system. Whereas in Guatemala's western highlands, the word milpa means something quite different. In a practical sense, the milpa concept is built around the Three Sisters framework (see below), and has a deeper philosophical and spiritual significance rather than a scientific one. In this spiritual system, the most important thing is to live in harmony with the complex web of life forms. To live well in nature, rather than dominate it from the outside.

The Three Sisters - traditionally corn, beans and squash – are grown together in raised beds, often with chilies and other complementary plants. The Milpa/Three Sisters system hinges on the special relationships between these plants: Corn offers a vertical platform for the beans to climb. The beans - clever and robust nitrogen fixers – use this platform to rise above the other plants, draw nitrogen from the atmosphere and convert it to essential nutrients. Squash grows out around the base of the corn, beans and chili and keeps unwanted competition from growing there. It also keeps the soil moist and prevents erosion. Flowers from the various plants attract a range of important insects, which in turn play complementary roles in this system.

Each part of this complicated system functions for its own benefit and survival, and for that of the whole. Together, the beans, corn, squash and chilies create a very sustainable environment, which ultimately generates many of the essential nutrients humans need to survive. Compare this to a large mono-cropped cornfield, for example, which depends on complicated chemical intervention, abstract marketing systems and specialist labor.

The Three Sisters/Milpa system brings to life the saying 'small is beautiful' and strongly influences AMA's approach to organizational structure, programming and networks, which aim to address issues in the most sustainable way on the micro and macro levels.

NUTRITION AND AMARANTH

After collaborating so beautifully in the garden, the various amino acids provided by corn and beans form an almost complete protein at the table. Interestingly, amaranth was another essential food in ancient Maya civilization, which had high cultural and nutritional value. Amaranth contributed high protein quality, with its high levels of Lysine - the missing link in the Three Sisters' protein-amino acid mix.

The dramatic reduction in the production and use of amaranth has been attributed to restrictions imposed by the Spanish after conquest. Once the conquerors learned of the grain's profound spiritual significance. Although it is often considered a poor man's food, amaranth – both its grain and leaves - once played an important role in balanced Indigenous diets.

STAPLES

GUATEMALAN REFRIED BLACK BEANS
Serves 8-10

INGREDIENTS

1 lb black beans

6-8 garlic cloves, finely chopped or crushed

2 medium onions, chopped finely

1½ tsp. salt

2 Tbsp. oil

6 oz. queso fresco (a white cheese that crumbles easily)

PREPARATION

1) Wash and drain the beans, picking out any stones or debris. Place in a large pot and cover with cold water until the water level is 2 inches above the beans. Soak overnight.

2) The next day, drain beans and discard water. Cover with fresh water until the water is 2 inches above the beans. Add the garlic, and bring to boil. Turn the heat to low, cover the pot and simmer for 1 hour.

3) When the beans are tender, add the onions and salt. Simmer for 30 minutes to an hour. Taste the beans and adjust seasoning to taste. More salt may be needed.

4) Drain the beans, reserving the cooking liquid. Heat oil in a large skillet. Add the beans and around ½ a cup of the reserved liquid. Mash the beans, adding more of the reserved liquid, as needed. Stir until the puree thickens and the liquid evaporates and the beans are a soft and smooth consistency. When served, crumble the cheese on top.

STAPLES

RED BEANS WITH SPINACH AND RICE
Serves 10-12

INGREDIENTS

For the beans:

2 ½ lbs of red beans

1 ½ bags of spinach

1 ½ lbs of onion

1 ½ lbs of tomato

1 head of garlic

1 tbs of cumin powder

1 tbs of ground black pepper

2 tbs of corn oil

4 bay leaves

For the rice:

1 ½ lbs of rice

1 lb of julienned vegetables

½ lb of peas

2 finely chopped onions

3 tomatoes

3 tbs of oil

PREPARATION

1) Boil the beans the day before, without salt so that they are ready to cook quickly. Cook them with an onion and a head of garlic.

2) Chop the onion and garlic and sauteé them until they are translucent, then add the bay leaves.

3) Then add the beans, tomato, cumin, and pepper. Cook for 14 minutes, meanwhile, wash the spinach appropriately.

4) When the spinach is ready, tear it with your hands and add it to the bean mixture.

Rice Preparation:

1) Sauteé the onion and vegetables together, add the rice when the vegetables become translucent and cook for 15 minutes, while moving the mixture constantly.

2) Later, add the water and salt, cover, and leave it until the rice fully absorbs the water and careful not to over boil.

STAPLES

ATOL DE ELOTE
Serves 8-10

Guatemalans are accustomed to taking hot beverages, known as atoles, which are made from a base of ground maíz and water. Other ingredients are added for flavor, including amaranth, anise, honey, pumpkin seeds, cacao or bean to name a few.

INGREDIENTS

5 ears corn

3 cups milk, divided

1 cup of panela or 1/2 cup honey (add at the end)

2 cinnamon sticks (about 3-inch long)

1 pinch kosher salt

PREPARATION

1) Use a sharp knife to remove the kernels from the corn and place them in a blender.

2) Add 1/2 cup milk and puree until completely smooth (2 - 3 minutes).

3) Transfer the mixture to a medium pot, add the rest of the milk, sugar, cinnamon sticks, and salt. Stir.

4) Bring to a boil over medium high heat, stirring constantly. Then reduce heat to medium low and simmer, still constantly stirring, until the mixture is slightly thickened (about 15 minutes).

Serve hot.

THE TURKEY AND PEPIAN

Pepian is an important traditional Guatemalan dish, which can be made with chicken or turkey.

Because the turkey symbolizes both gratitude and welcoming, Pepian made with turkey is seen as particularly special. It is often prepared and eaten when a man plans to ask for a lady's hand in marriage. When a man has this intention, he visits the woman's house to ask permission to 'date' her. Later, when it feels like the right time to take things to the next level - and propose 'tying the knot' - the man cleans a turkey well, places it on a generous nest of fruits and vegetables in a basket and presents this gift to the family of the potential bride-to-be.

This important gesture is, however, the culmination of many, mindful steps, which would have begun months earlier: The turkey would have been carefully selected at market. The man's family would have cared for the turkey and spoken to it with love. They would have done all this in the faith that their words would be transmitted to the bride-to-be and her family when they finally ate the turkey, and that this transmission would strongly influence the future union. Essentially, the turkey must feel the love that the man feels for his future wife and her family.

If the family accepts the man's offer (which he is usually quite confident of before presenting the turkey), they will also have a great responsibility. The family will need to take great care when cooking the turkey: The bird must be extremely tender when served, but it is also vital its bones do not break, and the bird does not fall apart. This is because the care that is taken with the turkey is symbolic of the care that must be taken with the new union and, in fact, all relationships. This subtle culinary dance is also performed in the spirit of community being more important than the individual, and the idea that great care needs to be taken in the way we treat each other.

THE TURKEY AND HUIPILES

The turkey is represented in the traditional clothes' designs of some Guatemalan regions. Large turkeys, chickens and people holding hands, for instance, appear on the huipils of the women of San Juan, Sacatepequez, near Guatemala City. If a woman is wearing this type of blouse she will transmit a message to the local people, who have knowledge of the meaning of these symbols, that the woman could be engaged to be married.

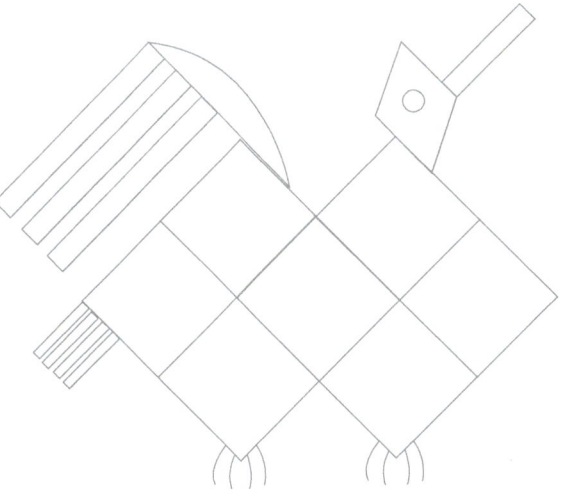

STAPLES

PEPIAN
Serves 8-10

INGREDIENTS

3 lb chicken cut into pieces, or use chicken thighs, which have the most flavor

3-4 cups chicken broth

1 1/2 teaspoons salt

5 medium-sized roma tomatoes

5 medium tomatillos, husks removed

2 medium onions, skin on

4 large cloves garlic, in skins

½ cup sesame seeds

1/4 cup pepitas (shelled pumpkin seeds)

2 sticks canela (the softer, easily shredded type of stick cinnamon usually found with Mexican spices, not the hard stick cinnamon)

1/2 teaspoon red pepper flakes or to taste

1 pasilla chile

2 guajillo chiles

1 ancho chile

2 corn tortillas

1/2 teaspoon achiote powder or paste

1/4 teaspoon black pepper

PREPARATION

1) Place chicken, broth and salt in a large pot and bring slowly to a boil. Reduce heat and let simmer until the chicken is cooked through, but not quite fork tender (about 20-30 minutes).

2) While the chicken is simmering, put tomatoes, tomatillos, onions and garlic on a large cast-iron or nonstick skillet. Turn the heat on to medium and let the vegetables dry-roast for about 15 minutes. When they are soft and roasted, move them on a plate where they can cool enough to peel.

3) Put the sesame seeds, pepitas, cinnamon, and red pepper flakes in pan over low heat. Toast them, tossing occasionally. Once you can see them browning, remove from the heat and pour into blender.

4) Now toast the pasilla, guajillo and ancho chiles, turning them a few times for a few minutes. Take them off the heat and turn onto a plate. Now, toast the tortillas until they are crisp.

5) Put the spices, tortillas, and dried chilies in the blender (after removing stems and seeds) until a powder. Adding a cup of broth may make this easier. Next, trim stem ends and skins from the cooled, pan-roasted vegetables and tomatoes. Add to blender until this forms a smooth sauce.

6) Serve pieces of chicken on a plate covered generously with the sauce, or serve stew style in a bowl.

CHILES RELLENOS

Serves 8-10

Serves 8-10

INGREDIENTS

For the sauce:

4 large tomatoes
1 chile huaque or 1 chile de arbol
1/2 red bell pepper
1/2 onion
1 garlic clove

For the chiles:

10 poblano or pimiento chiles
1/2 lb mozarella cheese thinly sliced
2 carrots
1/3 lb green beans
3 medium potatoes
1 small white/yellow onion
2-3 cloves of garlic
2 springs of thyme
1 bay leaf
Capers (as much/little as you like)
2 table spoons of balsamic vinager- olive oil
salt and pepper to taste

(Note that the ratio of veggies to pork is 1 to 1)

For the batter:

5 eggs
1tbs of flour

PREPARATION

For the sauce:

1) Boil all ingredients above with a cup of water until tomato starts to break. Discard water and liquify.

2) In a bit of olive oil, add the liquified sauce, season with salt and pepper to taste and cook uncoverd for about 5 minutes.

For the chiles:

1) Make a "t" insicion and take the seeds out leaving the stem in place. Then roast the chiles on stovetop until partially charred. Place in covered bowl to remove skin easily later.

2) Mince the carrots, potatoes, green beans. Finely chop onion and garlic

3) Chop onions, and garlic and cook for 3 minutes, cool and set aside to add to the vegetable mixture later. Add capers, thyme, vinegar, bay leaf, salt and pepper. Cover and cook at medium/low heat until veggies are tender

4) Finally add tomato sauce just enough to have a juicy, not dry, stuffing.

5) Stuff chiles (you may need a couple of toothpicks to prevent the stuffing from coming out) with vegetable mixture and sliced cheese.

For the batter:

1) Beat the egg whites in a bowl until nearly frothy, then add the yolks and a bit of all purpose flour.. Beat the ingredients together.

2) Preheat 2 cups of oil, submerge chiles in egg batter and fry until golden . Transfer the chiles to a paper towel to capture the excess oil.

Serve with tomato sauce and parsley on top

AMA SUSTAINABLE AGRICULTURE
PROJECT SNAPSHOT

Three generations of women arrive in a flurry of artisanal color and good humor, and it quickly becomes clear they are ready to get their hands dirty, despite their glorious traditional wrappings. The group, from the highland community of Espumpuja - aged between one and 65 years - have come to participate in a program that has been co-organized by AMA and Arizona-based sustainable agriculture experts, Kim and Joe Costion. The program aims to teach and reteach organic growing practices to Guatemalan farmers, and help them regenerate, often badly damaged, farmland. The course will also remind them about the great importance of maintaining natural heirloom seed banks and using these seeds over patented, chemical GMO seeds. One lady stoops to plant onion seedlings with a baby secured to her back in the traditional way. A vibrant textile square wraps around her and her baby the way maíz leaves wrap themselves around the cobs. The toddler is clearly accustomed to seesawing between horizontal and vertical positions. She plays with her mother's headdress, watches her every action intently, and eats what is passed to her.

To date the women have learnt to make 'walls of water' (rings of water-filled plastic tubes, which protect tomato and other seedlings from the elements), and developed their knowledge of companion planting. Today will be a full day: The women will practice making 'lasagne' beds, they will make and use concentrated compost 'soup', and learn how to construct cloth and hoop tents to protect their plants from frost in the cooler months. They will also learn how to train plants to grow upwards on the steep inclines, which characterize this land. Lasagna garden beds are made by alternating layers of organic matter with layers of soil, and release nutrients in much the same way nature does. "The food breaks down slowly, and releases nutrients gradually - not like chemical fertilizers, which release fast and sometimes burn the plants," said Kim. The women's productivity and enthusiasm have seen eight terraced beds constructed in the past week, rather than the planned two. The mismatch of traditional huipils and trajes from this and other regions is both breathtaking and strange in this indelicate atmosphere of toil. Kim and Joe plan to return later in the week for a vital discussion about seed-saving. "I want these women to understand how important it is to keep their traditional seeds," said Kim. "Not just for them, but for the world. These heirloom seeds continue to produce year after year, unlike the hybrid, chemical ones they are being pressured to buy. The new seeds stop producing after one year, whereas the heirloom seeds keep yielding and, moreover, are an important part of tradition and culture that cannot be replaced if lost. "We consider seed-saving to be critical to farmer freedom," said Kim.

"The majority of rural farmers in the Western Highlands use GMO patented seeds, which are illegal to save from one planting season to the next. As a result, farmers are forced to buy new seeds annually." This cycle perpetuates rural poverty and dependency on big agricultural distributors that are increasing their monopoly, and destroying the land more and more each year. Seed-saving prohibition also runs contrary to centuries of traditional agricultural practice.

Heirloom seed-saving has never been more important, as agricultural giant, Monsanto, wrestles with the Guatemalan Constitutional Court (at early 2015) over the further expansion of agricultural property patents. It is for these reasons that AMA introduced its sustainable agriculture program and has plans to expand the program to be a school for instructing communities on how to be more productive and sustainable in their principle economic activity.

PLANTING RITUALS
CALLING FOR WATER AND GOOD ENERGY

At the spring equinox, when the star representing Venus is bright in the sky, many Indigenous Guatemalan families ask permission of the earth to plant their annual crops.

Following a good rain, the family walks into the cornfield to smell the wet earth and connect with nature. They pray for a good harvest and focus on drawing good energy and guidance into the seeds they will plant on the day of Q'anil, meaning seed, and what they yield. The family also prays for enough water to nourish the seeds, their plants and the earth. This ritual, the smell of rain, and thoughts of future harvests, give people a strong appetite, so once the pre-planting ceremony is finished the family leaves the field to enjoy a special meal in their home. This is comprised of wheat tortillas and a hearty beef stew. The Maya believe this broth and the wheat tortillas nourish 'the worm in the stomach' while the corn grows; sustaining it, and them, until harvest time.

WHEAT TORTILLAS

Wheat tortillas are generally only made on special occasions - such as just before the planting – or when the year's maiz supplies have been exhausted. (For many of the poorest families, with limited land or resources, this often happens after about ten months). Wheat tortillas are delicious and substantial and can make you very thirsty. This is because wheat is heavier than cooked maize and requires more digesting. For this reason, you need to drink alot of water with them.

Serves 4-6

INGREDIENTS

2 of cups whole wheat flour

1 tspn of baking powder

1/2 tspn of salt

2 tbsp of olive oil

1/2 cup of warm water, more or less as needed

PREPARATION

1) Combine flour, baking powder and salt then add olive oil and stir until well combined.

2) Next add the warm water a few tablespoons at a time until the dough can be gathered into a ball.

3) On a floured surface, knead the dough by hand for about 10-15 minutes. Cover and let rest for about 15 minutes. Divide the dough into 10 balls.

4) Roll each ball to form a circle on a floured surface to make sure the dough does not stick.

5) Cook each tortilla on an ungreased skillet over a medium-high heat for about 1 minute, 30 seconds on each side, until it has some colour and puffs up a bit.

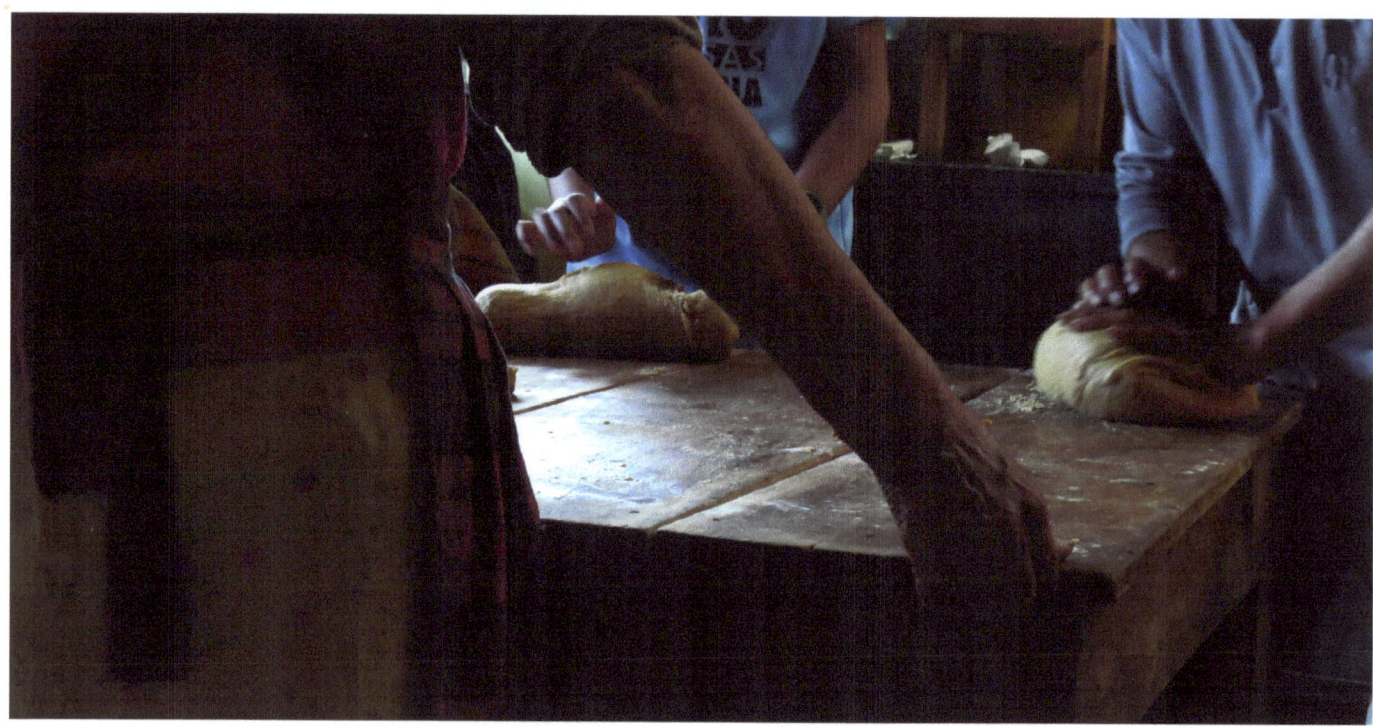

PLANTING

WHEAT AND EXCHANGING BREAD

As previously mentioned, many Maya traditions have been interwoven with Christian beliefs and practices since Spanish occupation. This blending of different systems accounts, in part, for the abundance of baked goods and wheat products during certain important events, such as Semana Santa (Easter) or those following the death of a loved one.

Wheat is a rich Christian symbol, with a number of biblical significances: In many Bible parables wheat and weeds are metaphors for believers and non-believers, respectively. Wheat and the Holy Communion wafer also symbolize the Body of Christ, as explained in this Bible quote from Jesus: "I am the living bread that came down from heaven. If anyone eats of this bread, he will live forever. This bread is my flesh, which I will give for the life of the world."

The exchange of rich breads between guests and hosts is a strong Easter tradition, based on the principles of community and sharing what one has. At one time, many days were spent baking and kneading in the home, although today families are more likely to place orders with local bakers, with available income determining the richness of the bread. The exchange of bread is also an important aspect of the rituals surrounding death, when carefully prepared bread and other food are regarded as gifts to the living from the deceased. Thus, getting the funereal food right is considered a very important aspect of honoring one's loved ones.

ARROZ GUATEMALTECO

Serves 6-8

INGREDIENTS

1 measuring cup of long-grain white rice

1 tablespoon of oil

Half a finely chopped onion

1 clove of minced garlic

½ a finely diced red bell pepper

1 very finely diced carrot

1/2 a finely chopped tomato

A pinch of ground cloves, if you can find them

A large pinch of salt

Freshly ground black pepper

2 cups of chicken or vegetable stock

1/4 cup peas. If you've bought them fresh from the market, blanch them first until nearly tender.

PREPARATION

1. Heat the oil in a frying pan and sauté the uncooked rice in the oil for around a minute or two so all the rice is glistening.

2. Add the onion and sauté for another couple of minutes.

3. Add the garlic and sauté for a minute. Then the bell pepper, carrots, and tomatoes and sauté, for another minute.

4. Finally, add the clove powder, salt, pepper, and the stock and stir well. Bring to a quick boil, lower the heat, and simmer covered until most of the liquid is absorbed and the rice is cooked (15 to 20 minutes).

(Don't be tempted to stir the rice. It will cook through and it shouldn't burn on the bottom if it's over a low heat)

5. Add the peas (if using), turn off the heat, cover, and steam the peas with the residual heat until cooked. Fluff the rice and vegetables with a fork right before serving.

This recipe is perfect as an accompaniment for Jocón or Pepian or simply vegetables.

MAYRA'S BEEF BROTH
Serves 4-6

INGREDIENTS

2 lbs beef, with or without the bones

1 güicoy, a type of zucchini or squash

2 güisquil (also known as Chayote in Mexico)

1 yuca or cassava

2 carrots

1 lb of potatoes

2 corn

1 lb of onions

1 bunch of cilantro

1 lb rice

PREPARATION

1) Boil the beef until tender with 1 chopped onion, several pieces of cilantro and a couple of pinches of salt. When the beef is cooked thoroughly maintain the broth and put it to one side.

2) In a large pot of water, cook each vegetable one at a time, because all the vegetables have different cooking times. Once cooked, remove each vegetable from the broth, before cooking the next one.

3) Once all the vegetables have been cooked, add them all to the vegetable broth with the chopped potatoes, the remaining onions finely chopped, the chopped cilantro - about 1/2 cup – with stalks removed.

4) Combine the beef, the beef and vegetable broths and cooked vegetables in the one large pot. Simmer for 15-20 minutes.

5) Garnish with cilantro, serve with wedges of lime and wheat tortillas for dipping into the delicious soup.

AGRICULTURE, THE SILK BELT

Guatemala is situated in the middle of the Silk Belt, a very fertile ribbon of land that circles the globe just above the equator. Many countries inhabiting this region share a variety of characteristics: They are often economically very poor and, thus, referred to as 'third world' or 'developing' nations. Many are, however, unaware that these nations are also some of the richest places on earth, according to other measures. Crops that cannot be grown in other parts of the northern or southern hemispheres can be grown easily here due to exceptionally high levels of rain and sun. Whereas, no matter how hard farmers in Nebraska, Normandy, the Ukraine or Japan, for instance, try, they cannot produce coffee, bananas, cardamom or other 'tropical' products, with the same ease or on the scale they are grown in the Silk Belt - if at all.

Another striking feature – and sad irony – of this region is that, despite an abundance of lucrative food crops, large segments of Silk Belt populations suffer from malnutrition and hunger. This is because much of what is grown is sent for sale elsewhere. In Guatemala, for example, the wealthiest 2% of the population controls 68% of all land. This group also almost exclusively controls the country's most fertile and productive land, and grows sugar, African palm (for bio-fuels) and fruits, all almost exclusively for export. The Silk Belt is also home to a large number of Indigenous people, which live in Nation States they did not create. Nation States ruled by people who share linguistic, cultural and racial ties with people of the global North. Silk Belt countries continue to suffer frequent military and political interventions with the purpose of maintaining the same land use patterns, which marginalize millions of poor and malnourished First Nation people. The poverty issue in the Silk Belt is, therefore, not about a lack of resources, but resource distribution.

CUTTING THE FIRST LEAVES
MID-WAY BETWEEN PLANTING AND HARVEST

June is a wonderful time: The corn has sprouted its first leaves, the cobs are taking on recognizable forms like healthy embryos, and there is generally a spirit of celebration in the air. And this optimistic spirit about the coming harvest often manifests in a fiesta or two. At the mid-harvest point, we cut the first leaves from the adolescent corn stalks so that the soil's nutrients are drawn into the maiz rather than its foliage. But before the first leaf is cut, we have a ceremony to give thanks to the earth for what it has and will give to us. The greenery from the maiz is also traditionally used to make two dishes - Jocón and tamales. Jocón is a special meat stew and the maiz leaves add color and nutritional value to the dish's green sauce or gravy.

At mid-harvest, the maiz leaves are also used to make tamales. A corn leaf is wrapped around some raw corn dough – called masa – to make a small parcel that is steamed to make the tamale. At other times of the year, tamales are often wrapped in banana or platano leaves. But in June, they are wrapped with corn leaves, which lend a special mid-harvest flavor to the tamales. If there is spare money, a family will make meat broth to go with the tamales, and once the latter have been eaten, the leaves are collected and gathered in bunches for hanging in the house as a memorial of what the earth has provided.

Tamales were said to have been created as a portable food for Maya armies, hunters and travelers somewhere between 8000-5000 BC. Tamales can be sweet or savory and when resources allow, they might have cheese or meat at their center.

Maya women have wrapped their babies to their bodies with vibrant textile cloths for centuries, in the same way a maize leave wraps a corn cob.

TAMALES
Serves 6-8

INGREDIENTS

Masa
3 ½ cups corn flour
2 tsp. salt
1 ½ tsp. baking powder
10 Tbs. cold vegetable shortening
1 cup low-sodium vegetable broth

Filling
3 poblano chiles
2 Tbs. olive oil
1 medium onion, chopped (1½ cups)
⅔ cup golden raisins
½ cup low-sodium vegetable broth
½ tsp. dried oregano
1 cup pitted green olives, sliced
8-9 inch maíz/banana leaves

Romesco Sauce
6 jarred piquillo peppers, drained (½ cup)
3 Tbs. sherry vinegar
1 Tbs. smoked paprika
½ cup roasted almonds
¼ cup plain breadcrumbs
4 cloves garlic, peeled
½ cup olive oil

PREPARATION

1) To make Masa: combine corn flour, salt, and baking powder in bowl. Add 2 1/4 cups hot water, and beat on medium speed until mixture is crumbly. Increase speed to medium-high, and alternately add shortening and broth 1 Tbs. at a time. Beat 15 minutes, or until mixture is light and fluffy. (To test texture, drop 1 Tbs. masa into cold water. If it floats, it's light enough.) Set aside.

2) To make Filling: Preheat oven to broil. Place chiles on baking sheet, and broil 8 to 10 minutes, or until blackened on all sides, turning occasionally. Place in bowl, cover with lid, and steam 15 minutes. Pull off charred skin by hand, and dip chiles in water to remove blackened bits. Remove stems, seeds, and veins, and cut chiles into 1/2-inch dice.

3) Meanwhile, heat oil in skillet over medium heat. Add onion, and cook 10 minutes, or until browned. Add raisins, broth, oregano, and chopped poblanos; simmer 5 minutes. Remove from heat, and stir in olives. Cool.

4) To assemble tamales: Hold each maíz/banana leaf square briefly over low gas burner to soften. Place each maíz/banana leaf square shiny side up, atop 10-inch foil square. Spread 1/2 cup Masa in thin layer over center third of each leaf. Top with heaping 1 Tbs. Filling. Fold over sides and then ends of banana leaf to enclose filling in Masa, then wrap in foil square.

5) Stack tamales in steamer basket, and steam over simmering water 1 hour, or until Masa is just set and pulling away from banana leaves.

6) Meanwhile, to make Romesco Sauce: Purée peppers, sherry vinegar, and paprika in blender until smooth. Add almonds, breadcrumbs, and garlic, and purée until smooth. With blender motor running, add olive oil in steady stream until smooth sauce forms.

7) To serve: Remove and discard foil from tamales. Serve with Romesco Sauce.

MID-HARVEST

JOCÓN

Serves 6-8

INGREDIENTS

2 1/2 to 3 lbs of chicken pieces

1 1/2 cups of chicken broth

4 cups of water

2 tsp of salt

1/4 cup pumpkin seeds (pepitas)

1/4 cup sesame seeds

2 corn tortillas, chopped, soaked in water, drained

1 cup of tomatillos, peeled and chopped

1 bunch of cilantro, chopped

1 bunch of scallions, chopped

1-5 jalapeños or serrano chile peppers, chopped

PREPARATION

1) Place the chicken, water and salt into a large pot over medium-high flame. Bring to a boil, reduce heat to medium-low and simmer for 30 minutes to 1 hour.

2) Remove the chicken to a bowl and strain and set aside the broth. Let chicken cool, then remove the meat from the bones and shred it with your fingers. Set aside.

3) Heat a dry skillet over medium flame. Add the pumpkin and sesame seeds and toast, stirring, until lightly browned. Remove to a coffee grinder and grind to a fine powder.

4) Add the sesame and pumpkin seeds, tortillas, tomatillos, cilantro, scallions and chile peppers to a food processor or blender. Add 1 cup of the reserved broth and process until smooth. If using a blender you may have to do this step in batches.

5) Add vegetable broth to pureed ingredients to give it a more sauce-like consistency. Heat over medium-low flame and simmer for an additional 15-25 minutes. Adjust seasoning, add tofu and crema, and serve.

CALDOS
BROTHS AND SOUPS

As well as being nourishing, soups and caldos are excellent ways to utilize the leftovers and bits and pieces that families have in the pantry, particularly when stores are lean.

One special broth that is commonly prepared by midwives incorporates the herb, apazote. Apazote restores a new mother's strength and contains high levels of vitamin K, which is excellent for healing wounds. The broth's salts and fluids and the nutrients from other vegetables and available meats, also build up the mother's energy, electrolytes and general reserves before and during breastfeeding.

MID-HARVEST

CALDO DE PLATANO
Serves 4-6

INGREDIENTS

1 tablespoon extra virgin olive oil

1 small onion, finely chopped

1 carrot, finely chopped

1 rib of celery, finely chopped

2 garlic cloves, minced

4 -4 1/2 cups of vegetable stock

2 green plantains, peeled, quartered lengthwise & thinly sliced

1 bunch cilantro, stemmed and finely chopped

1/2-1 teaspoon cumin

1 bay leaf

salt & pepper

PREPARATION

1) Heat oil in large saucepan over medium heat.

2) Add onions, carrots, celery and garlic. Cook, uncovered, for 3-4 minutes, or until onions are soft but not brown.

3) Add 4 cups of chicken stock/broth and bring to boil over high heat.

4) Add plantains, most of the cilantro (reserve a few tablespoons for garnish), cumin, and bay leaf. Season with salt and pepper. Return to boil.

5) Reduce heat to medium-low and simmer, uncovered for 40-50 minutes or until plantains very tender. Remove and discard bay leaf.

6) Transfer half the soup to blender; puree until smooth. Return to the pan.

(If soup is too thick, add a little more stock/broth.)

Season with more salt/cumin if desired.

CALDO DE RES
Serves 8-10

INGREDIENTS

2 lbs of inexpensive beef (with bones)

olive oil for browning beef

1 small tomato, with an 'x' cut in one end

1 small onion, with an 'x' cut in one end

3 whole celery stalks

1 whole bell pepper, seeds removed and halved

1 yuca root, peeled and cut into chunks (or frozen if not avalaible)

1 whole carrot, peeled

3 huisquiles (mirliton, chayote)

3 corn on the cob (or frozen if not available)

1 small head cabbage, quartered

2-3 whole small potatoes, scrubbed

Seasoning

1/4 cup of chiltepe chiles (dried or fresh)

1/4 cup of diced onion

1/4 cup of chopped cilantro

juice of 1 lemon

PREPARATION

1) Brown beef in oil in a large soup pot, add vegetables. Add enough water to almost cover vegetables. On high heat, bring everything to boil.

2) Reduce heat to low, add seasoning to taste. Simmer until vegetables are cooked and beef is tender. (about 40 minuites to 1 hour)

Note: You may add or substitute vegetables with whatever you may have on hand– platanos, greens, root vegetables etc.

3) Toast chiltepes on a fry pan, then put in mortar and pestle and break them up. Add diced onion, chopped cilantro, and lemon juice. Mash briefly, just to blend the flavors.

Serve caldo over rice, garnish with cilantro. Serve chiltepe sauce on the side.

MAKING DO, AND MAKING FOOD LAST

The more remote a community, the more precious food and rationing harvest produce tends to become. Add to this the fact that highland communities all over the world are predominately populated by Indigenous people, who in turn, suffer disproportionately higher levels of poverty and marginalization. Add to this the facts that, in the past, refrigeration was very limited or non-existent and markets only opened on Sundays, so anything bought there, especially meat, had to be prepared in a way that would make it last for at least a week. Therefore, traditional Maya families have had to be very clever about finding ways to make food last well and longer - much like people setting out on a long sea voyage many centuries ago. Now markets are open on many more days, sometimes daily, and produce is more readily available. But poverty persists. The recipes that have evolved from the challenges mentioned above often involve salting, fermentation and pickling and are still popular today. More often than not, they also make food tastier!

Cultural note: Western highland families always have food ready for planned or unexpected visitors, especially during festive periods like Semana Santa (Easter) or Christmas. So preserved food can come in very handy in this way too!

MID-HARVEST

ESCABECHE

A pickle served as an accompaniment to caldo, frijoles, eggs or guacamole.

Serves 8-10

INGREDIENTS

4 heads garlic

1 1/2 lbs of carrots

1/2 lb of peas

around 15 shallots

1 cup of vinegar

10 bay leaves

2 lbs of jalapeños

5 branches oregano

4 cups apple cider vinegar

1 cup water

PREPARATION

1) Heat the oil in a frying pan and sauté the uncooked rice in the oil for around a minute or two so all the rice is glistening.

2) Add the onion and sauté for another couple of minutes.

3) Add the garlic and sauté for a minute. Then add the bell pepper, carrots, and tomatoes and sauté, for another minute.

Serve as a condiment as needed.

MID-HARVEST

CURTIDOS RAPIDOS

Served as a salad or to accompany rice or a main meal
Serves 8-10

INGREDIENTS

1/2 red cabbage, cored and finely shredded

1 large carrot, finely shredded

1 red onion, halved lengthwise and thinly sliced

2 fresh jalapeños, stemmed, seeded, and minced

1/2 cup apple cider vinegar

1-2 limes, juiced

1/4 cup finely chopped cilantro

1 tbs of local honey

1/2 teaspoons grated orange zest

1/8 tsp of ground allspice

1/8 tsp of dried oregano

PREPARATION

1) Combine cabbage, carrot, and onion.

2) Pour boiling water over mixture and then strain.

3) Put mixture in a large bowl and toss with jalapeños.

4) Whisk together vinegar, oil, lime juice, cilantro, honey, zest, allspice, oregano, 1 tsp salt, and several grinds of fresh pepper.

5) Pour dressing over vegetables and toss well. Refrigerate at least 30 minutes or, preferably, overnight.

MID-HARVEST

WATER

St John the Baptist Day, June 24, is the time to celebrate and give thanks for water. Without water we would not have harvests, or any life form for that matter, so it is extremely important to give thanks for this precious element. Our gratitude and hopes for good rain are expressed through prayer, and by decorating pilas, washing troughs, and water harvesters - and in the past - communal faucets.

HOW THINGS FALL APART
PLANTING A PATH FOR THE WATER AND THE WIND

Don Felipe Ixcot, a Mam elder from San Juan, Ostuncalco, recounts a story from the 1960s when Peace Corps volunteers from the United States arrived in his village to provide training in 'modern' agricultural techniques. Don Felipe's father argued that what was being proposed was not in balance with nature. That planting in rows just a few inches apart would only do harm to the water. The Mam way was to plant in mounds with plenty of space between the seedlings, leaving a path for water to travel through. Don Felip's father was also concerned that the tall corn stalks would not survive if planted in straight lines like a wall. 'Where would the wind pass?', he implored.

Don Filipe shared that while his father and grandfather instinctively distrusted the new techniques, he jumped in with both feet and finally convinced his elders that they should move with the times. The Americans, he explained, had science on their side and were getting amazing results with their new techniques and chemicals for killing weeds and increasing yields. Don Felipe recounts how proud he was in the first months of the experiment. How the new variety of corn grew much higher, and how optimistic he was about greater returns. What he did not predict was the tall variety of maize could not withstand the fierce mountain winds, which whip through the highland valleys.

Today, almost everyone in the village regrets yielding to those persuasive arguments for chemical farming, but they are finding it difficult to go back. Each year the soil is more damaged and the crops need larger amounts of chemicals to yield anything. Companies and their representatives continue to distribute free GMO seeds, which produce what some call 'killer crops', and affectively sterilize plants. It is easy to identify GMO-contaminated plants in the cornfields. Their crowns are now very pale, rather than the traditional vibrant, daffodil yellow.

HARVEST
TAPIZCA

Harvest time is calculated by counting 260 days from the day the corn seeds were placed in the earth. In Tejutla, and many other western highland communities, harvest is celebrated in a number of ways, the main ones being with a feast on the first day of harvest and the creation of an altar in the home.

To make the altar, a family must first search the cornfield for a particular kind of maíz; one that is comprised of all four maíz colors - yellow, a rusty red, charcoal and an ivory white. When a cob contains all the colors of corn, it is considered sacred and representative of the four cardinal points or directions. The leaves and silk of this special cob are peeled back to create a cape for a doll figure that is placed at the center of the altar. The altar acknowledges and symbolizes the four directions, and is a gesture of gratitude for what the earth has provided the family for the coming year.

To prepare for the harvest feast, the men in the family go to market to find a nice young sheep and once the altar has been prepared, the family performs a ceremony to ask permission to kill the animal for the feast. Both the altar and ceremony recognize the vital force of maíz, the sacred, staple crop.

At harvest, the men pick the maíz, the women pick the beans, then a ceremony is conducted to thank the earth for what it has grown for the community.

TORTILLAS, A CELEBRATION OF LIFE

In Guatemala and the rest of Central America, the most common use for maiz is for the omnipresent tortilla, and it is difficult to pass a cuadra or block without encountering the rhythmic ritual of tortilla-making. Maya culture celebrates life at every opportunity. This is done through music, dance, ceremonies, enjoying time spent together as families and communities, through food and in the simple act of making a tortilla.

We believe that each tortilla's shape reflects the sphere of the universe and tortilla-shaping is, in fact, a kind of dance. Before making the tortilla dough, or masa, the maíz first must be soaked in a solution of Calcium Hydroxide. This process, called nixtalation, makes the tortillas tastier, easier to digest and more nutritious, because it helps the body optimize biotin. Both the nixtalation process and tortillas originated in Mexico in pre-Colombian times.

CORN TORTILLA

Variations: We have already talked about wheat tortillas, which are served at planting time or when maíz stores have been consumed. Cornflour tortillas are another variation, which are commonly prepared as special Christmas treats.

Serves 4-6

INGREDIENTS

2 cups of corn flour

1 3/4 cup of water

1/4 tbs of salt

PREPARATION

1. Begin by mixing the corn flour with the water and salt. Add the water gradually and push the mixture around to completly wet the flour to form a dough.

2. Mix ingredients until you have reached a play-dough consistency. Remove a small piece, and roll dough into a small ball.

3. Shape the tortillas by hand, by "clapping" the dough. Clap the dough until the tortilla is flat, thin and circular in shape. You can also use a rolling pin or a tortilla press.

4. Cook both sides of tortillas in a pre-heated skillet over medium-high heat. Cook until golden-brown.

5. Remove cooked tortilla and place in a basket or a covered dish to keep warm.

RADISH AND CITRUS SALAD

Serves 4-6

INGREDIENTS

1lb of radishes, trimmed and sliced into thin rounds

1/4 cup of mint, finely chopped

1/2 cup of fresh orange juice

1/4 cup of fresh lemon juice

salt and pepper (to taste)

PREPARATION

1. Mix all together the ingredients together in a bowl and chill well before serving

One popular variation of this salad adds (2 cups of) chopped chicharonnes, fried pork rinds, which transforms it into a salad known as chojin.

ESTOFADO AND WEDDINGS

While Estofado is the Spanish word for 'stew', in parts of the western highlands it is associated with a substantial, slightly sweet meat dish that is frequently served at weddings, and other important events, such as fifteenth birthdays. (As mentioned previously, the other two main special occasion dishes are Pepian and 'Jocon'). Unlike Pepian, where the sauce is thickened with a paste of seeds and tomatoes, an Estofado utilizes the crumbs of a traditional biscuit. As well as providing body, these crumbs add a wonderful sweet balance to the Estofado's rich meaty and spicy flavors. Indigenous weddings are commonly considered important opportunities for the bride and groom's families to get to know each other and strengthen the ties between them. The families first share the marriage ceremony and a carefully prepared meal and once the main meal is complete, there is drinking and dancing into the night. Although, the latter takes place in a slightly different style to what you might expect:

A bride's aunt or cousin or brother, for example, might approach the seated uncle, brother or cousin of the groom, by taking a seat across from them and raising a glass of the local liquor. The person being toasted will know that this toast is also an invitation to connect in another way. So once the pair has taken a drink, they will move to the dance floor to move to the music without words or touch, but facing one another. This respectful dance is another metaphor for the marriage union, and the importance of getting to know and accepting one another with patience.

ESTOFADO
Serves 4-6

INGREDIENTS

- 2 lbs of beef chuck roast -cubed
- 4 cups of water
- 1 tsp of salt
- 1/2 tsp of pepper
- 1/2 cup of raw rice
- 1 tbs of flour
- 1/2 cup of graham cracker crumbs
- 1/4 tsp of achiote
- 1/4 cup of cider vinegar
- 1 tsp of thyme
- 1 small onion - thinly sliced
- 2 cloves of garlic - finely chopped
- 1 large tomato - sliced
- 2 whole cloves
- 1 Stick Cinnamon
- 2 Medium Bay Leaf

PREPARATION

1) Cook beef in water on a low to medium heat with salt until soft for about 1 hour.

2) Remove beef and reserve 3 cups of the broth.

3) Prepare a smooth sauce in the food processor with the rice, flour, bread crumbs, achiote, vinegar, thyme, onion, pepper, garlic and tomato.

4) Add sauce to the beef with the cloves, cinnamon, and bay leaves. Add 3 cups broth and simmer over low heat for a further 1 hour.

Serve with tortillas and rice.

THE CARDINAL POINTS OR FOUR DIRECTIONS

A fundamental aspect of Maya astrology and its cosmovision are the concepts of the four cardinal directions, and the idea that one must always know the location of the centre in order to live a good and harmonious life that is in balance with the universe and those around you. The four directions correspond to the concepts of North, South, East and West, and a vertical axis runs through the middle of these points, and between the zenith and the nadir. This vertical axis was represented in the Popul Vuh, when the First Father raised a ridgepole to lift the Sky up from the Earth. Each direction is said to exert a different quality, rhythm, energy and color and is vested with varying degrees of importance at different times in the Maya calendar and growing season. The eastern direction, where the sun rises, is the primary cardinal direction, whereas, the southern point signifies harvest and is, therefore, considered more important at this time.

THE HERO TWINS AND MAÍZ

In the Hero Twins story, "the Creators, Heart of Sky and six other deities including the Feathered Serpent, wanted to create human beings with hearts and minds who could "keep the days." But their first attempts failed. Then these deities finally created humans that could talk out of yellow and white corn, they were satisfied. In another epic cycle of the story, the Death Lords of the Underworld summon the Hero Twins to play a momentous ball game where the Twins defeat their opponents. The Twins rose into the heavens, and became the Sun and the Moon. Through their actions, the Hero Twins prepared the way for the planting of corn, for human beings to live on Earth, and for the Fourth Creation of the Maya."[1] In Maya oral tradition, maíz is usually personified as a woman, whereas in classic written mythology, a distinction is made between two male forms: a foliated (leafy) maíz god and a 'tonsured' version, which has its foliage stripped away. The latter maíz god is often accompanied by the Twin Heroes, which many scholars speculate to be the maíz god's offspring. Also, according to classical mythology, the Hero Twins have maíz plants for alter egos. Because of these strong connections with maíz, it is common for many Indigenous people in the western highlands to pay tribute to the Hero Twins at harvest time.

1 http://maya.nmai.si.edu/the-maya/creation-story-maya

DULCES
SWEETS

Sweets, dulces in Spanish, have played an important role in Maya culinary history for centuries. Honey, cacao and panela – an unrefined form of sugar cane that became popular in Latin America after Spanish conquest - have been the most common ingredients and sweeteners used in traditional *dulces*. While cacao-based chocolate has probably been the world's best-loved sweet for the past few centuries, the cacao seed actually began its culinary life as a bitter, spicy drink that was made from a fermented mixture of water, spice and ground, roasted cacao beans.

The Maya variously mixed cacao with maíz, chili, honey, peanut butter, different flowers and vanilla, but it was not until the sixteenth century, when the Spanish brought sugar cane to Latin America and paired it with cacao, that modern chocolate was born and introduced to the world soon after. Cacao, which originated in Guatemala about 4,000 years ago, makes regular appearances in Maya mythology: Hunahpú gave cacao beans to the Maya people, after humans were created from maíz by the grandmother goddess, Ixmucané. Cacao was used ceremonially by the Maya, who venerated the cacao tree. Similarly, chocolate was considered a food fit for the gods, due to its coveted medicinal and aphrodisiac qualities. Cacao beans were also used at various times as a currency.

The cacao god, Ek Chuah, is celebrated each April. This occasion was once marked by the sacrifice of a cacao-coloured dog, among other offerings.

DULCES

MANGO PUDDING
Serves 4-6

INGREDIENTS

6 tbsps of chia seeds

2 cups of unsweetened almond milk

3 tbsps of honey or panela

2 tsps pure vanilla extract

2 1/2 cups frozen mango

PREPARATION

1) In a medium bowl, mix the chia seeds and almond milk together and stir with a fork. Let it sit for 10 minutes and stir, breaking apart any large chunks. Let it sit again for another 5 to 10 minutes and stir.

2) Add the agave and vanilla extract and mix until well incorporated. Cover the bowl with plastic wrap and refrigerate for at least 4 hours. If you are planning to refrigerate this overnight, put the chia pudding in an airtight container and refrigerate.

3) When you are ready to eat the chia pudding, thaw the mangoes by immersing them in very warm water (the water should not be burning hot). About 10 minutes. Puree the mangoes in a food processor or blender.

4) Mix the pureed mango and chia pudding mixture together. Serve the pudding chilled and top with coconut shavings, lime juice, pumpkin seeds, or fresh mango.

CHOCOLATE BANANA BREAD

Serves 4-6

INGREDIENTS

3 ripe bananas

1/4 cup of raw honey

4 eggs

1/2 tbs of vanilla extract

4 tbs of melted butter

2 tbs of melted/softened coconut butter/coconut mana

3 tsp cinnamon

1 pinch of salt

1 tsp baking soda

1/2 cup of coconut flour

1/3 cup of mini chocolate chips

PREPARATION

Preheat your oven to 350 degrees.

1) In a large bowl add you peeled bananas and mash until they reach a paste-like consistency. (If there are a few small chunks remaining, that is fine.)

2) Add in the raw honey, eggs, vanilla extract, butter, and coconut butter and mix well, being sure to thoroughly combine the raw honey. You should have a very liquid-y batter at this point.

3) Grab a sifter and sift in the cinnamon, baking soda and coconut flour. Stir until just combined and then gently fold in the chocolate chips.

4) Line a metal loaf pan with parchment paper and pour in the batter.

5) Bake in a preheated oven for 55-60 minutes until the center is set. (Be sure to keeping checking your loaf.) When the center is set pull it out and let it rest for 5 minutes in the pan, then remove and slice. Enjoy!

DULCES

THE ROYAL LADY
HONEY IN MAYA HISTORY

Honey has long been a popular sweetener, antibiotic and the key ingredient in fermented Maya mead. It is also considered sacred in the Maya belief system. The existence of Ah Mucen Cab, the god for bees and honey, demonstrates their importance in both the culinary and spiritual senses and the bee's vital role in the perpetuation of life, through plant pollination, makes it an important symbol in the cosmovision. The bee is also thought to connect us to the spirit world. For these reasons, man's relationship to the bee and the act of taking honey are considered equally sacred acts. The traditional Maya bee does not have a stinger and ancestors named their preferred bee species, Koli Kab, which translates as the Royal Lady.

There are some extraordinary stories, from the Yucatan, of bees being released en masse as weapons of war to overwhelm the enemy - to powerful effect.

HONEY VS SUGAR

The bee lives in synergy with other life forms. This is in stark contrast to the sugar cane industry, which relies on a mono-cropping system that depletes and pollutes the soil, and removes habitat for a variety of animals, and plant forms. The sugar industry has played a part in a great deal of political conflict in Guatemala, and has frequently been the motivation behind the forced removal of land from Indigenous people. Many have been enslaved to harvest sugar cane crops and many more were killed to maintain land monopolies in the hands of the wealthy few. The extent of sugar's grave effects on human health are only now coming to light and scientific studies are finding that sugar is a key cause of obesity, increased diabetes and hypertension rates and other ailments. These risks and impacts are only enhanced by the addictive nature of sugar in its refined form.

DULCES

CHOCOBANANAS
Serves 6-8

INGREDIENTS

5 ripe, firm bananas

150g of dark chocolate (the higher the cocoa, content the better)

1 tbs of vegetable oil

popsicle sticks

Toppings

You can opt for one or both of the toppings

¾ cup of finely chopped peanuts, ready on a saucer

¾ cup of crushed or chopped granola or your favourite kind of cereal, ready on a separate saucer

PREPARATION

1) Find a baking tray that will fit in your freezer and line with foil or Clingfilm.

2) Peel the bananas and divide each one into three. Insert a stick into each third to create a popsicle. Place all the bananas on the baking tray and put in the freezer for 30 minutes.

3) Now make the chocolate mixture. Break the chocolate into pieces and put in to a glass bowl with the oil. Melt the chocolate either in the microwave (stirring every 30 seconds for 2 minutes until melted) or in a bowl over a half-full pan of simmering water, stirring continuously.

4) Take each banana piece and dip into the melted chocolate. You may need to spoon the chocolate over the banana to make sure it is fully covered.

5) Once chocolate has started setting, roll the banana in the topping of your choice.

6) Carefully place the topped banana on the baking tray. Repeat with the rest of the bananas pieces until you've used all the ingredients

7) Now place the tray in the freezer and leave overnight. If you can't wait, try one after 2 hours; the banana should be frozen in the middle and the chocolate should be set.

DULCES

CANELLITAS DE LECHE
Serves 6-8

INGREDIENTS

1/2 cup of honey

4 cups of powdered milk

1 1/2 cans of condensed milk, sweetened

1 cinnamon stick

1/2 cup of panela

PREPARATION

1) Place the ingredients, except the cornstarch, in a stand or hand mixer with a paddle attachment and mix on low for 30 seconds. Change the mixer to medium speed and mix for approximately 1 minute or until mixture has a stiff consistency.

2) Place the sugar mixture on a clean work surface, dusted with a bit of cornstarch. Knead the dough for a minute with your hands, using a dusting of cornstarch to prevent sticking.

3) Roll or pipe the mixture into 24 desired shapes, dusting with a little cornstarch as you go.

4) Wrap the shapes in cellophane or other desired wrapping for serving or gifts.

DULCES

PLATANOS EN GLORIA
Serves 4-6

INGREDIENTS

4 ripe platanos (roughly working out one per person)

1 cup of orange juice (preferably a bag of the freshly squeezed stuff for extra goodness)

15-20 cloves (roughly 5 cloves per plantain)

1 tbs of butter or 'margarina'

2 'ramitas de canela'

2 tbs of honey

PREPARATION

1) Melt a large tablespoon of butter in a frying pan. When the butter has melted, add the whole, peeled platanos and begin to fry

2) Stick 4-5 cloves into the flesh of the plantain. Break the two 'canela' sticks in half and add them to the pan so the flavor infuses into the butter. Start to lightly brown the plantain over a low heat, turning to fry on all sides. This should take around 10 minutes

3) Once lightly brown on every side, take the plantain out of the pan and sit on una servilleta or paper towel to soak up some of the oil. Leave for a couple of minutes to cool. Take the cloves out of the flesh and cut the plantain into slices, not too thin.

4) Put the pan back on the heat, add a drop of oil or more butter and start frying the plantain slices. Pour over the OJ. After a couple of minutes, drizzle half of the honey over the plantain slices. Then flip the platanos over and add the other half of the honey.

5) To make sure they caramelize, leave the platanos for about 5 minutes on each side. Spoon some of the juice over occasionally so it soaks into the plantain. The sauce should become thick like caramel. You can always add more OJ if you think you need more

6) Once cooked, turn the heat off and leave to sit for a minute or two in the pan. Serve with a dollop of cream or ice cream and a sprinkle of canela.

DULCES

EASTER SWEET BREAD
Serves 6-8

INGREDIENTS

Bread
1½ cups of lukewarm water

1½ tbsp granulated yeast (2 packets)

1½ tbsp coarse sea salt or kosher salt

8 eggs lightly beaten

1/3 of cup honey or panela

1½ Cups unsalted butter, melted (3 sticks)

7½ cups all purpose flour

PREPARATION

1) Mix the yeast, salt, water in the bowl of your mixer, mix well.

2) Add in eggs, honey and melted butter, and continue to mix until well blended.

3) Add in flour and using your dough hook, incorporate all the flour, mix just enough so that all the flour is mixed in.

4) The dough may look loose and wetter than you think it should be, it may also look like it has lumps, that's ok.

5) Transfer dough to another bowl, cover with a towel and allow to sit and rise for two hours. Chill dough for at least 2 hours, before making the rolls*

6) Cut out twelve 2 oz pieces of dough, using floured hands roll each piece into a ball, by pulling the dough down and around, pulling it tight at the bottom.

7) Place dough ball on baking sheet and continue the process until all are done. Cover with a towel and allow to rise for 30 minutes. Preheat oven to 375 degrees

8) Bake for 20 minutes or until the roll is a nice deep golden brown.

MIEL DE GARBANZO

This dish is normally prepared at Easter time in Guatemala and, while there can be a number of recipe variations as each family adapts the dish to available ingredients and personal taste, sweetness from canella and fruits, and the starchy element of chickpeas which absorb the syrup, tend to be the common denominators.

Serves 6-8

INGREDIENTS

2lbs chickpeas

1lbs of panela

2 plantanos

2 acorn squash cubed

1 1/2 cinnamon sticks

skin of one orange, in one continuous piece

PREPARATION

1) Cover the chickpeas with water and bring to them to the boil. Simmer for 10 minutes then drain and rinse, removing the skins. Place back in saucepan covered with fresh water and cook till al dente.

2) Chop the platanos, without removing skin, into 2 inch pieces and simmer gently till tender. Remove skins and put to one side.

3) Cube the acorn squash, removing skin and seeds, and add to chickpeas, boil until it is tender through.

Each family personalises this sweet fermentation to their own preferences and budget. The unnegotiable foundation of the recipe is generally chickpeas, sugar and cinnamon, served with pastry, which is often crumbled on top. Although, I have heard of at least one example of a family that removes the chickpeas and prepares a medley of poached seasonal cinnamon fruits instead.

THE DAY OF THE DEAD, NOVEMBER 1ST

The Day of the Dead is a time for remembering and reconnecting with family members and loved ones who have left the physical world. The rituals carried out around this day – now a fusion of Catholic and Indigenous traditions - remind us of the coexistence between the living and the dead. Celebrations start the night before the Day of the Dead, when an altar and special meal are prepared in the house. The next day, western highland families visit their ancestors at the cemetery, taking sweets, alcohol and kites. Many also prepare a traditional meal called Pixan. Pixan is the force that animates us, the energy and spirit that propels the body and this dish is eaten beside one's ancestors' graves. The alcohol is passed around and sprinkled on the graves and family members in a cleansing ceremony of remembrance; the sweets are enjoyed and left for the ancestors, who - it is well-known - adore their *dulces*. The sky is filled with the moving color of large and small kites, made from crepe paper and bamboo. Kite-flying on this special day is about breaching the gap between physical and non-physical realms, and playing with one's ancestors in the nether space between them. In many communities, the kites are burned at the end of these celebrations as a signal to the dead that it is time for them to return home. Many believe if the kites are not burned, the souls will not return, and those who mourn them will not be able to move on with their lives. The Day of the Dead is not the sombre occasion one might expect. Children walk and run freely on and around the tombstones, going where the kites and wind lead them, and food and drink are enjoyed by all in this unexpected setting. Indigenous cemeteries in Guatemala and Mexico are often brightly painted, joyful places. This is because the Maya have a different attitude to death and time, seeing the latter as circular and without beginning or end. The vale between the two worlds is, therefore, felt to be very thin, so dead ancestors can visit the physical world, and some gifted individuals have the ability to make the crossing in the opposite direction.

"I look at the German section of our cemetery - so gray, bleak and sad – with its iron fences to keep people out. I never understood that. Many of us natives wonder about Christians who see death as so final and fear it so much, despite believing in an afterlife... Of course, we are sad when a family member passes to the other side, because we will miss their daily presence. But, we also know they are present in our memories, and we will still be able to communicate with them... My mother has two spirit helpers, which take the form of birds. I know they sometimes visit me when I am having difficult times far from home. The birds bring my mother's presence to me and messages from her."

Guadalupe Ramirez

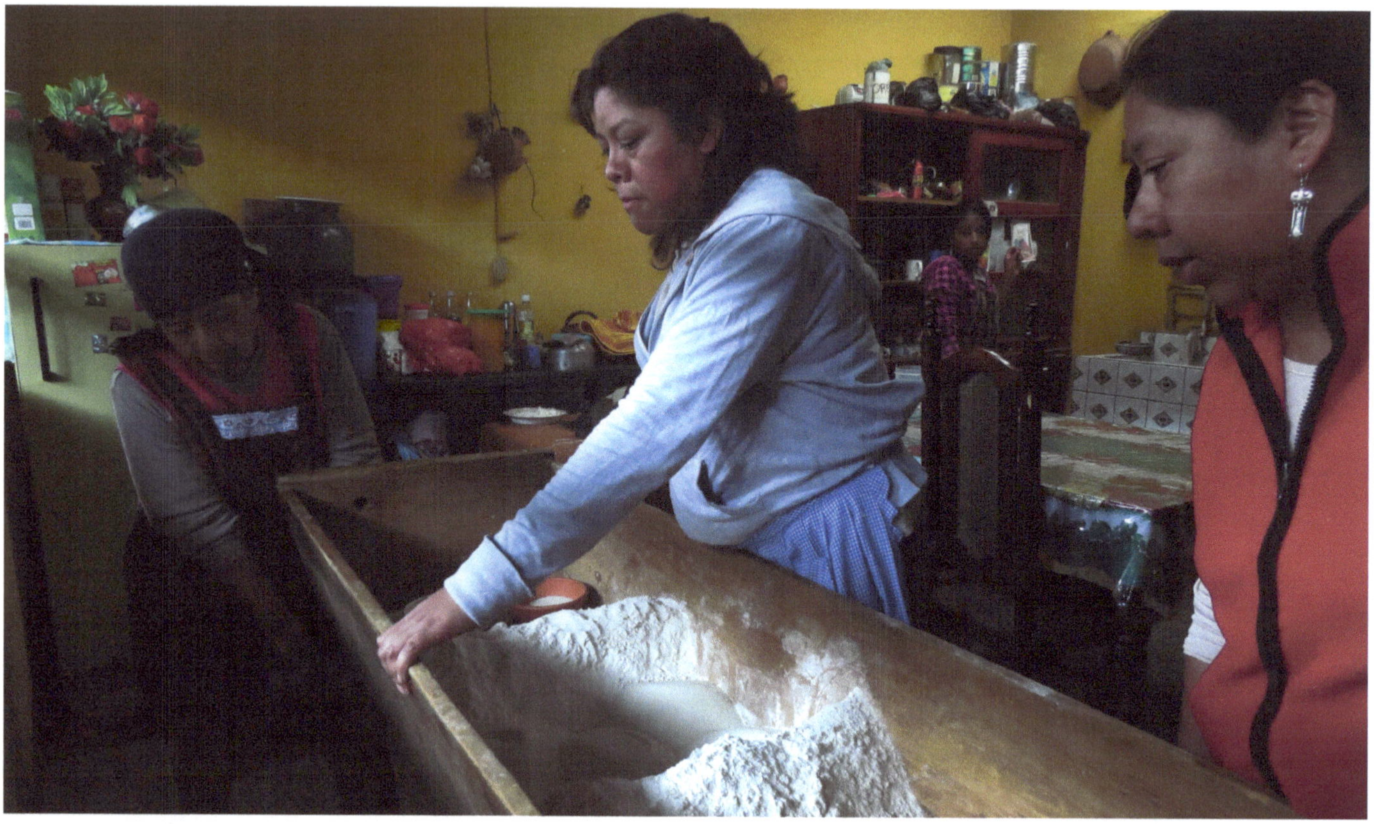

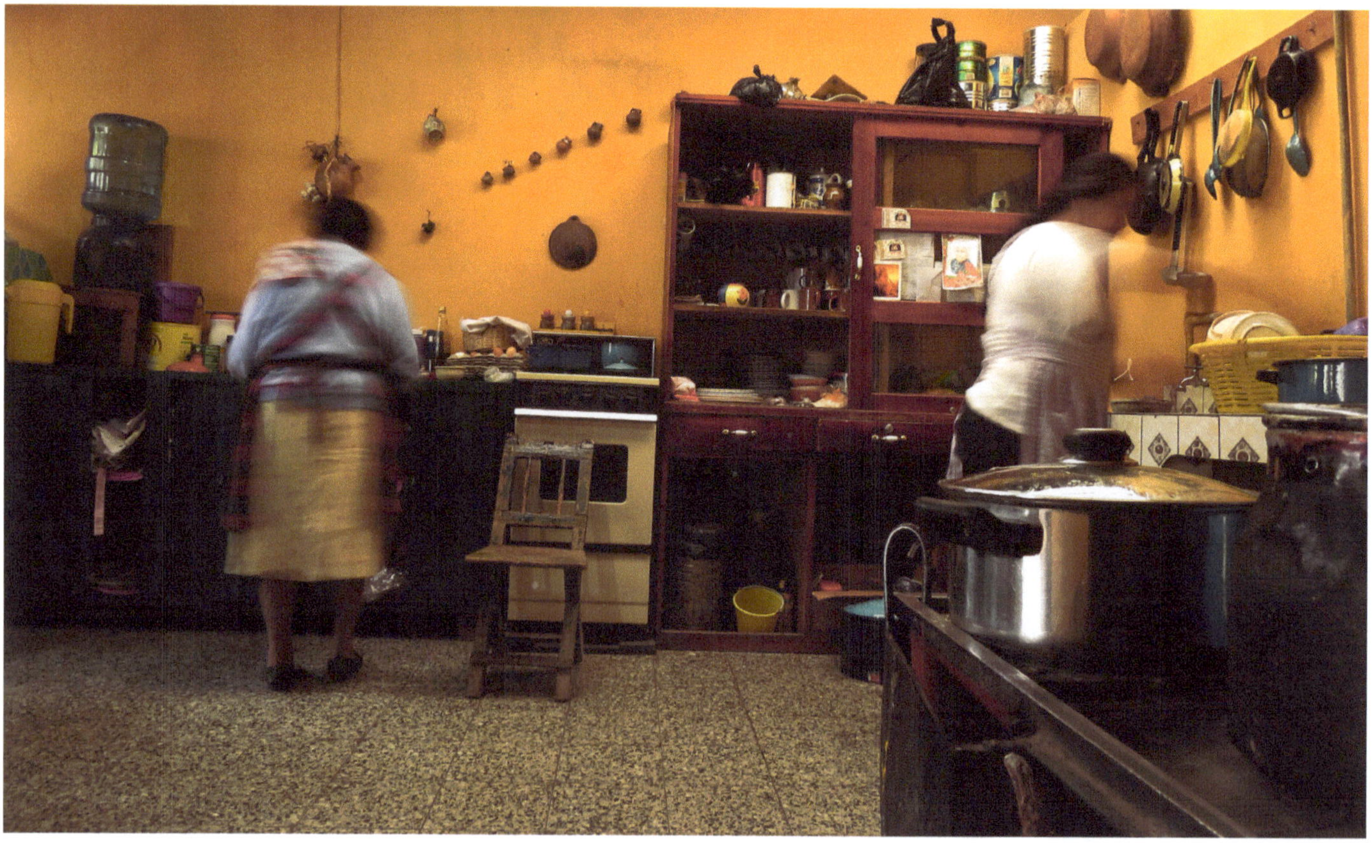

LUNCH AND CONNECTION
THE HIGHEST CURRENCIES
GUADALUPE RAMIRÉZ

In Guatemala, lunch is the principal meal of the day and in my western highlands community it continues to be an un-negotiable and unhurried daily ritual. For us, lunch is a time for families and friends to sit down together and share food, recipes, the day's activities, and gratitude for the things they have. In keeping with our worldview that the best learning comes more from experience rather than from books, we believe that some of our most important learning happens over lunch. Indeed, kitchens - where people exchange stories and knowledge between mouthfuls - are the real classrooms. Lunch is also the medium through which relationships are built and strengthened, and relationship, in my experience, is the highest currency in traditional indigenous communities - much more prized than money or material things. For all of these reasons, hurrying lunch to return to work or some other 'more important' task is unheard in my community - because there is no more important task! In keeping with this importance, if a highland family invites you to share food it has prepared, it is a generous and meaningful gesture, and acceptance of this invitation is considered equally meaningful. The latter indicates a mutual desire to share time and, often precious, resources with your hosts, and an acceptance of them as people.

All these ideas connect with another idea I would like to leave you with: Food's value and enjoyment is completely and utterly affected - be it enhanced or diminished - by the manner, environment and company in which it is consumed. If you eat something quietly in front of a lake, in good and present company, it will taste completely different from when it is eaten in front of a computer or next to a busy road. This may seem like an obvious thing to say, but I believe it is a truth that is fast being forgotten - despite its importance for our personal and communal wellbeing. Finally, in the spirit of this book, I would like to wish you many, many, happy and tranquil meals with loved ones into the future.

RECOVERING FOOD SECURITY
IN THE GUATEMALAN HIGHLANDS

Food insecurity is a critical issue in the Guatemalan western highlands. Guatemala has the highest national level of chronic malnutrition (48.9 percent) in the western hemisphere and the fourth highest in the world. Food insecurity is most severe in the highlands where drought is recurrent and many people eke out a living from non-irrigated subsistence agriculture. In AMA's partner communities, 70% of children suffer from malnutrition, and the rest of the population has climbing rates of diabetes and high blood pressure. These communities are experiencing an influx of western food companies like Coca Cola, Frito-Lays, and McDonald's, accompanied by intense advertising instead of education about healthy alternatives or the negative effects of these new foods. Additionally, food handouts from well-intentioned international charity organizations make it very difficult for local farmers or traditional barter economies to survive. Overall, is seeing longstanding knowledge about health, traditional cooking, and organic agriculture slowly forgotten and displaced by fast food culture. AMA first became involved in food security issues when two women's groups, in Llanos del Pinal and Santa Catarina, identified this as a crucial issue in their communities. AMA has subsequently worked to empower Maya women's groups by developing new and traditional strategies for healthy living in the face of rapid social, economic and cultural change.

The Highland Support Project continues to support AMA's agriculture and healthy eating programs. This includes building greenhouses with visiting Highland Partner teams, coordinating agriculture and seed saving classes for women's groups, and the development of an agriculture teaching curriculum with the support of agronomists Jo and Kim Costion from Northern Arizona. Additionally, community members are trained in water collection, as Water shortage is a significant challenge, and women often need to walk an hour or more each day to collect water for their gardens and homes. Our collective, long-term vision is to expand the established greenhouse infrastructure, diversify crops, and continue increasing and retrieving sustainable knowledge and practices, which will be passed on to the next generation and allow our partners to produce enough food to achieve true food sovereignty.

Adapted from words by Ben Blevins

AMA SUSTAINABLE GARDENING
PROJECT SNAPSHOT

Three generations of women arrive in a flurry of artisanal color and good humor, and it is quickly clear that they are ready to get their hands dirty, despite their glorious traditional wrappings. The group, from the highland community of Espumpuja, aged between one and 65 years, have come to participate in a program, which is co-organized by AMA and Arizona-based sustainable agriculture experts, Kim and Joe Costion. The program aims to teach and reteach organic growing practices to Guatemalan farmers, to help them regenerate their, often badly damaged, farmland.

The course will also remind them of the great importance of maintaining natural heirloom seed banks and using these seeds over patented, chemical GMO seeds. One lady bends to plant onion seedlings with a baby secured to her back in the traditional way. A vibrant textile square wraps around her and her baby the way maize leaves wrap themselves around the cobs. The toddler is accustomed to see-sawing between horizontal and vertical positions. She plays with her mother's headdress, watches her every action intently, and eats what is passed to her.

To date, the women have learned to make 'walls of water,' rings of water-filled plastic tubes that protect tomato and other seedlings planted from the elements. The women have also developed their knowledge of companion planting. Today will be a full day: The women will practice making 'lasagne' beds, they will make and use concentrated compost 'soup,' and learn how to construct cloth and hoop tents to protect their plants from frost in the cooler months. They will also learn how to train plants to grow upwards on the steep inclines that characterize their land.

Lasagna garden beds are made by alternating layers of organic matter with layers of soil and release nutrients in much the same way nature does. "The food breaks down slowly, and releases nutrients gradually - not like chemical fertilizers, which release fast and sometimes burn the plants," said Kim. The women's productivity and enthusiasm have seen eight terraced beds constructed in the past week rather than the planned two. The mismatch of traditional huipils and trajes from this and other regions are breathtaking and strange in this indelicate atmosphere of toil.

Kim and Joe plan to return later in the week for a vital discussion about seed-saving "I want these women to understand how important it is to keep their traditional seeds," said Kim. "Not just for them, but for the world. These heirloom seeds continue to produce year after year, unlike the hybrid, chemical ones they are being pressured to buy. These new seeds stop producing after one year, whereas the heirloom seeds are do not and, moreover, they are an important part of tradition and culture that cannot be replaced if lost.

A teenage boy with a pick helps the women with the tougher digging and, during a pause, he plucks a white lily from the ground, stares at it for some minutes, and when the baby starts getting restless, instinctively, hands it to her. "We consider seed-saving to be critical to farmer freedom," said Kim. "The majority of rural farmers in the Western Highlands use GMO patented seeds, which are illegal to save from one planting season to the next. As a result, farmers are forced to buy new seeds annually."

This cycle perpetuates rural poverty and dependency on big agricultural distributors that are increasing their monopoly, and destroying the land more and more each year. Seed-saving prohibition also runs contrary to centuries of traditional agricultural practice. Heirloom seed-saving has never been more important, as agricultural giant, Monsanto, wrestles with the Guatemalan Constitutional Court (at early 2015) over the further expansion of agricultural property patents. It is for these reasons that AMA introduced its sustainable agriculture program and has plans to expand the program to be a school for instructing communities how to be more productive and sustainable in their principle economic activity.

Partner with us to continue fortifying these programs and advancing the cause of native resilience. Together, we can help communities continue to thrive without having to abandon their ancestral lands and their communities. Re-establishing indigenous methods of cultivation and harvest is not only beneficial to the earth, but strengthening and affirming to the spirit and self-esteem of historically marginalized native people. Our sustainable methodology allows communities to break chains of dependency on outside aid and major companies' local dominance; so that they can be healthy and happy with the connected relationship to their food that we all deserve.

Were you fascinated by the rich culture of traditional foods presented in this cookbook?

Join us on an Indigenous Food Ways Journey

 **FACEBOOK.COM/HIGHLANDSUPPORTPROJECT**

 **HIGHLANDSUPPORTPROJECT.ORG**

www.ingramcontent.com/pod-product-compliance
Lightning Source LLC
Chambersburg PA
CBHW042022150426
43198CB00002B/39